Birds and Fancies

Also by Elizabeth Treadwell:

Poetry
Chantry (Chax Press, 2004)
LILYFOIL + 3 (O Books, 2004)
Cornstarch Figurine (Dusie Books, 2006)

Prose
Eleanor Ramsey: the Queen of Cups (SFSU, 1997)
Populace (Avec Books, 1999)

Chapbooks
Eve Doe (becoming an epic poem) (Double Lucy Books, 1997)
The Erratrix & Other Stories (Texture Press, 1998)
Eve Doe: Prior to Landscape (a+bend press, 1999)
The Milk Bees (Lucille Series, 2000)
LILYFOIL (or Boy & Girl Tramps of America) (Duration Press, 2002)
Mub or the false transgressive evangelista (Furniture Press, 2006)

ELIZABETH TREADWELL

to Holly
thank you for

Birds and Fancies

being our teacher.
see last poem
for a music
together quote.

love Charlotte

&

Shearsman Books
Exeter

Published in the United Kingdom in 2007 by
Shearsman Books Ltd
58 Velwell Road
Exeter EX4 4LD

www.shearsman.com

ISBN-13 978-1-905700-16-5

ISBN-10 0-905700-16-4

Acknowledgements
Some of this work first appeared in the chapbook *mub or the false transgressive
evangelista* (Furniture Press, 2006) and in the periodicals *Barrow Street,
Chain, Court Green, Dusie, Foursquare, Freehand, mem, P-queue, Shearsman,*
and *Women's Studies Quarterly.*

Dates of composition: May 2003-May 2006.

Immense thanks to my husband, Paul Jackson.

The publisher gratefully acknowledges financial assistance for its 2005-2007
publishing programme from Arts Council England.

Contents

for Ivy Rae Jackson

Long legged waders
(or A History of English verse)

in cabbage-rose;
or the mercy & glorie of *Halcy.*

after Myles Coverdale

Yes us will mix a lot, in palace glare, next quiet pool. Next a
pond by *Halcyon* us low & crie; flung us upon the trees, required
a songe. Next us recall did *ye*, o fancy one, as for our chords.
Now us will mix a lot, the Lordes sweet songe, forgotten here,
in an odd spot. Now us will mix a lot, if to no more, let no roof
mouth.
Remember, yes, in the day us say. Oh daughter *thou* shalt
grounde & playe, in these sweet days, happy happy shall you be,
dressed like the sea, in cabbage-rose. In cabbage-rose.

byrdys

"Gode Ivy, what
 byrdys ast thou?"
—Anonymous, 15th c.

the days swim by guilelessly
—in the rainstays,
pressed like the blooms
song-bright, loose, disjointed
apostrophe to the sun
o shifty, your dark rosy crown
—a day finch & some day pigeons,
gulls, geese, quackers,
stubby hummers, &c (little
one on ones, a branch
in a tree) —scrubjays, crows,
bufflehead, troopscout—
the lone western tanager
as we prepared for your birth

The Whistle Trees

> "From here, it takes so many stamps
> to post the most modern researches."
> —Lorine Niedecker

farhouse slides whistleblow the curtail
trinkety & slovenly, gentleman motorist
in the carnal meeting-hall, the candied rainbow—
awash, afield, mid-boulevard
the whistle trees
roll by

Velour Séance

in memes & clutches everyday,
folded underhill
such monument & yoyo
bric-a-brac the scene,
in variance & cluster
sasses who, the queen?
in nary flash & hapless fawn
everlope marine

Sugarcoat

chestnut backed chickadee
pink ape
the large oak site
of your birth

Halloweentown

With the first storms come
new birds, some lift black
wings, parade a little band
of red; some are seabirds
from the interior
bearing ancient silver mazes
on their good drab chocolate
backs; crisp &
prim a sherbet moon
stands out in deep blue
silks above our stubby
housetop, like a frozen
mango scoop; set amongst,
under the blood moon,
we blow kisses, you in
your furry uniform,
me my flimsy shirt.

The false transgressive evangelista

(i.)
until the world needs women again,
I live in the woods with my sons:
the saints' talents, and the birds humming
and the birds not humming,
under the bone tree,
by the dinghy, the oaks dark
against the gold.

the new usual,

the empty word-hut.

sometimes nasty witnesses,
the resort colts, mine & others'
shell-bright memoirs—
here in this landscape we've bitten—
the original lawlessness;
low-rent trees
in the foreground
(we're advised to hire more trees).

the big-wig carry-all of yore;
that large, differing hand;
sweet, flip echoes
(his thousand petticoats).

storm choirs with simple english,
the sacred follow-up.

(sleep like riverbanks holding us in.)

the cruel laws of the throne,

undone the churchstep:

(ii.)
the prison of no past,
a christ in every literature.

the floating grimace
of personal despair.
it's just perspective
that's all
it is

(thanks, thin goons of the mood police.)

in the curse lots
foreign words like little pets,
with genders,
& curls.

the little words step down,
garden-heavy
in the windows of a church—

rub the idealist,
the bulbous theme:

(iii.)
its face-splashed
news apparel,
homemade rotten filmstar,
or thuggy celebrity gelding.

the house motions
of animals at night,
like a character
stuck to a scene.

(these treetop hormones
older than   our brains.)

here in this landscape we've bitten
the train, the watertower,
& the mail. tender finger-stubs, offspring's
feats & qualities.

until the world needs women again,
I live in the woods with my sons.

the country moon, the fat orange jewels of winter;
all our gliding, loose particularities—

sweet protectorate,
and broody.

hummy

for Ivy

in tinky glass
stand, gather green
company, milky bud

3/3/04

butterfly

for Ivy

our rusty seashell props
the breeze, little hands
& dark orange wandering

(undated)

hospital

for Ivy

the hall of plastic & foam
you in the cradle of a tiny word

(firstborn)

chance is a grass sequinned
mine is a heart unpinned
for you are a love unend

family portrait at Stinson Beach, May

the very white sand
      and the very dark sand
all the middle sand
the orange sand and
   the beige sand
      and the brown sand
all my lifelong sand
the clay sand and the
   charcoal sand and
      the sea sand
the crystalline

Trod.

no ordinary gambit all these marriages
down in Soho under the bridge
daughter of cemeteries, factories,
sin . . .

i. manchester
transvaginal upon a diplomatic
spouse, culture of the court —
her parents' senator, his second,
which gives the ancestry

ii. song_b.htm
"What sullen star was't struck my fortune blind:"
The imprint is fictitious.
A narrative of a mob's raid of a brothel.
Cropped at head with loss of title;
I sheet; A slip-song— "Come all you parents that have children dear,"

iii. oakland
Event
Gothic, Stick/Eastlake
Area of Significance:
Period of Significance:
Owner: **Private**
Historic Function:
Historic Sub-function:
Current Function: Education, Vacant/Not In Use
Current Sub-function:

Mamie

What a song that I am singing
What a song that I have sung
Hear my voice it's in the singing
of the song that we have sung
What a song that I am singing
Hear this song
it is
the one

What a song that I am singing
What a song that I did sung
Hear the song it's in the singing
Hear your voice it is the one

What a song it is I'm singing
What a song it is I've sung

All the songs since the beginning
All the songs that we have sung

Hear this song that I am singing
Hear this song my little one

Sonora

i. in the path of likely growth

at least 500 species of birds
while the pores are kept open
a broad array of plant
but the threats
the continent
the nowhere else in the world

congress between scott and stone
waverly
country club
speedway
campbell —
nowhere else in the world.

on a hot day
you would not see
that man walking
down the street
with a buttoned-up collar
and tie

but the threats
the cardinal red
but the threats
all the little birds
the threats to their
to the survival of these,
resources
at rates rarely matched

alice, mary and blanche
two WWII vets
we'd have these
300 blocks of ice and you'd

open these doors on the side
of the railroad cars and put these
big blocks in there and the ice
water there and that was their
cooling system. I had that
job for awhile.

as with all southwest
as with the title
as little driest annually
as with, but despite

about mammals, 20 of amphibians, nearly reptiles, about fish,
            and at least birds.
plants too, the richest.

human occupation began prehistoric and then lapsed
a few tens of thousands until europe in the 16th
for several reasons, slowly remote

late in the road and rail, and the emergence of large-scale projects
            to control water
concentrated tends to concentrate
the sprawl disperses
subsurfaced the geographic limits of these cities, causing
            enormous

*

one house gives a turtle the run of the backyard,
a hundred year old parrot, & a lawn
catholic rescue mission on the shag

diversity is marked as well
if the number of life forms and the variety of ecological
although some indigenous
most notably
the region
the total

a combination tourism

*

what do injured, sick, or orphaned
on the easy,
there's the reasonable view that nature should be allowed to
    take its course.
on the, a distressed animal in your yard may not be a "natural"
    situation—for example, it may have been injured by a
    neighborhood cat.

ii. starmouth's mother

starmouth
all my little knowledge

& in this life I
have knelt & swayed
before the twin catholic women,
whose name means
bitter, longed-for
child.

(This I do no longer.)

iii. waverly
    for Grammy

into the global anxiety box
we put cigarettes, gumdrops, & dust;

ice chips; birthstones;

glasses of water

The imported ghost deer of Inverness, California

as if part of the fog they are steamy &
part of the fog
skimming the bulky peninsula
the dark grass & rock

sea-sandy, grass, root of tall thing;
sea-sandy, grass, earth, dark as the sea

Sourgrass

Surely ours contained
dog pee, likely bum pee
+ frat pee, why not shit;
litter & cigs; anything
else?

But it seemed so clean
pressed up against
the asphalt, its heads
swinging in the barmy
afterschool breeze.

Do kids even try
it these days?

Dinosaur Meat

shy gifty, I felt snubbed.

poetry's like a small dried sponge seeped in time,
tongued at leisure (in peril) at safety (in chains)

we press ourselves to the earth

The Clove-pink

In the milk-light
the clove-pink

I am unborn
crystal, meat

The sun pierces them
For they are our honeymoon curtains

"I feel renewed.
Pleased that my youth is
finally finished."

"No Mom!
Picture of little flower!

Picture of big flowers
Picture of big flowers, Mama"

the qualities of the seabreeze once it's defined the mother and
the child

on our walk
birds hop

torn flowers bathe
in a bed of leaves

hydrant & sidewalk are doodled
in black & pink hearts & skulls

driven into geologic time
next to kerosene shutters

on a warm rock with Dada
bathing in stars

in time's suburbs
Mama's haberdash memory

let's dress in media
consider the mirror

the big sparkly
shoes

coming down through years & climates
turning head, tenacious grip

how densely slippery

what sweet animals

Ladyless or Gayntyl Maydenys

The letters of Name are trellises for stars
All of what is is Name, & she sings Name, Name, Name
You are her gardenia, worn & inhaled
pure & a fragrance going out to the night.
—Alice Notley, "Beginning with a Stain"

As if responding to the traffic jams
which paralyze the city, History itself
seems jammed because all sorts of
propaganda machines cover up what's
true or what needs to be told.
—Etel Adnan, *Of Cities & Women*

In Cloudland

for & with my niece Violet

Through most of the story the little boy & girl are accompanied by a large spider as their chief guide in Cloudland, which the children are able to visit in their shared dreams.

Up alphabet hill
& down the shady
hard curved roads
of your tiny youth

How's it going,
Queen?

Stuffed animals crammed into the
Natural History Museum

for my sister Margaret

The Individual palaces
of masculine and feminine
have crumbled
are crumbly in our time

into the global wrecking crew
into the bewildering fire
the surreptitious claims

far a girl can walk herself to kindergarten these days
in most kinds of western weather
with a glimpse toward the dustbinny wishing well, perhaps a
            short peek
into the books & equipment

city doves

we are like birds, my love,
hand-painted,
large and strange
with twig-like limbs,
cawing at odd hours

for Paul

Little Bear

little expert
little witness
little star

Ladyless

after Alice Notley

my ancient credo
tossed round like decor

City Dove

egg-bound
on our tiny
busy stoop

mub

or curmbox: a purse poem

what is the job of the steady function?
the parchment of my debut
single curved switch
ascending track
maps of the torch membership, street market palaces, awards,
    nonedible groc.

tendered, shown two feet, brainiacs

plumage even clever, in their way. but for all impressive science
jarring avian today. experts switch wholesale. the first total
makeover century. the new asylum, which draws broad upon,
acknowledges twitchily, and, in many cases, primates cannot.
particular bulk reflects a new recognition, fully 75 percent
cerebral. accordingly, undersystem, no longer a part of that
region, with its Latin root. as of today it is the, the opposite of
sticks and stones — names do matter when it comes to think
"about things."

Buffalo 3000

17 times as high as the moon
being ladyless blows chunks
three literary combatants join forces with the ink bomb disposal:
the feminist lessons of regret, intolerance, &c —
overwork, and my unsubtle education in stability.
["Involvement rather than simple registration or the generations
        before." (Norma Cole)]
podunk & chico: archives fluidity, the golden-eyed . . .
        . . . clairvoyant mack if you're a ladyless boy.
modblog — random nursing: with over 100,000 vacant positions
        and a ever-growing need

daresay expires forward all the stuff naive or trivial.
More within one gendered I propose a possible topic, or
        something culture stages. don't know, plan to be there.

In the broken staring

after & for Philip Jenks

Eerie timing too. the passage and my if anything banging.
say to moved and bed. when if tossed your bright signature.
broken scribbles. filled perpetual flank. the timing was strange
thank you. different from the book. the body and pace and time
— know this is a snippet. walls and mattress, slit under field.
the song's collapse, decibels of want. the belly crafted cloth, in
bushes, orbs, how intermittent. unfolds the fold, how how.

vlur vain

out of the glittering homestead
notions of beauty so strict
she broke with the fairytale narration
spent it on elsewhere
all upon her analyzed dismissal
sinking strictly like a stone

the river is paved with them
in the crooks of our arms

gelatin

after the Duchess of Newcastle

within the house, kitchen boys
and scullery maids
collage the hooves, denatured
thoughts so variety rank in despair
a large body equipped
which not
have speech

historically, bovine or porcine
skin or bone
acid or base
extraction. approximately —
her theory liquid abuse —
suspected of plotting hospitality
consumed in some aspect of oral drug,
metric tons, and devices.

another five so dizzy armed us.
woodland lanced open to the bottom fragments
exhibit lot-to-lot furthermore.
route of your loyal willing.
the family's coach.

neither did suffer the symptoms.
probably vaccines and biologics –
new punctuation —
typical of disappointed courtiers —
composed of softer, colder, moister
treatment with exterior,
remedy close to the house.

by making formal "legs,"
a masculine manner,
whatever her wonder rather
to be seen than told.

gelling or non-gelling gelatins.
distinct molecules
currently used

Royaltronic

"little crime rate. little shoe."
— Joyelle McSweeney

scarcely does she sleep. scarcely does he wake.
she walks and walks and walks.
For the cold cameras.

Daughter holds your face
demanding to survive
these elements

this is not a toxic gumbo
this is not a First Lady

flame

"we are all full of diasporic shapes that have no memory"
— Renee Gladman
"inaudible as a flock of eggs"
— Melissa Benham

pocket witness,
the refractive liberty
of being brained embodied
then species anxiety

so we set sail,
lay anchor, and persist
slap slap against the belly of the shoreline

"oh the big ship sails on the alley alley oh"
— Mother Goose

dear double-handed,
double-fisted, pup

the daughters sing
in black & green & heather
in the small yard
the ancient sea-hut
by the overlarge & blue

in memoriam Richard Carscallen

The Clove-pink:
The Carnation Skirt/Pink druzy

The Carnation Skirt

knots of time & influence
space & dirt & flesh

"dirtsky"
"space dirt"

"watersky"
"milk"

it is who
it is
climbing
up

shape holy food

The Carnation Skirt

brown hat, brown dress, brown balloon
little kitten, little burr

Blogosphere

perhaps we are simply nervous shapes
knotted to the horizon, or merely
rickety pages crinkling ceaselessly

beneath fingers
jude law falls asleep
fully clothed, even shoes on
by the pool at the chateau etcetera

enter the drifty field
camp fallow –
follow any newby lead:
the sacred cow, the slowly worm,
the debutante, the mom pet

the male pundit the male pundit the male pundit

(in this poem
i am jude law)

Pink druzy

Tiny crystals cover the surface of this sparkling spitting out
of ancient names into the policy mumbo, brief ally, in the
postoscar dream of love, weaving an arrangement or riding a
tide—shy trinkets of the interior—little horses, little trams—a
dollhouse of a city—just begging to be embodied—shy field,
mini-causeway—beaded to infirm projections—or a central
casting negligee, 500 mini essays on usage—bullies—kissing the
ass—is it a butterfly or a moth? a butterfly or a moth? a butterfly
or a moth? —just begging to be embodied—crystals cover the
surface of this sparkling spitting—ancient names—kissing the
ass of the postavant, flarf this—fuck it. we've been wronged—&
I thought pink druzy would be such a sweet poem, full of love
for my daughter.

dandelion

these little rooms of clarity—
bright cellulose cubes, & we
move in them—
borne by the tides like sprites
& false things, a thousand
kissable projects

Temporary

call on Mrs Greensleeves—

it's sog:
the haunted dress, the other moons—
England like a pile of sticks
                    RESIST THE CONQUEST MAPS, THEM
it's sog, homebody:
the haunted dress, the other moons
corduroy . . .
            stumblejack eyes like planets steering?

al the blue the relations of the Indians
all the *Salvage* blue, heart pink i
adore ya

sog—
the haunted dress, the other moons
corduroy showing
the times what made me

*

the ghost year
Resist the false maps of conquest.
England like a pile of sticks.

Mrs Greensleeves

Foursquare compline

after Medbh McGuckian, for Jessica Smith

this is who is what is dowdy minstrels
at these point in time, we are all crossed
by mrs greensleeves
but her transparent house
mrs greensleeves
my haunted dress
with bitter candy

Poem beginning with a line from Medbh McGuckian and ending with an interjection from my daughter Ivy and in which the main character is myself renamed

Jennifer Suzette: But [my] transparent house
all these bitter years complaining
this or that was not quite
marionette
no! I want my sunglasses!
I already have my sunglasses
at my house

katie holmes's pacifier

the phony man sessions.
fabricate birdsong. assault ministry.

Blogosphere compline

if i don't allow technology to steal me
wolfing down the dreams
three skies – pink, blue,
& red – climb into this valley
climb into this flowered break
through these lumpy
clouds

turtletown compline (palimpsest)

fluid products of the humane, and one tendency

advocating doll sleighs

giving objects their due

certainly the elite, intellectual

makes much: robs the person described of her own

self-interpretation or mapping) to that which he himself wife,

sister, aunt, daughter, etc; no matter that she is stripped, as is

the "cavalier,"

it could be argued the lady at least wears a

distinguishing adjective, while it's hard to say. In fact even the

actions in this scene seem generic and fake. Thus the scene and

its people calcify,
>   the big, busy truth — not to mention
>   — the weather, etc. — brought into
>   terrible use

Clearly the "we" in this paragraph

which press inconveniently, beautifully, chaotically

against anyone's flatten, for example in the sand with "his foote

more to do with topography, land use, and social

relations than with Euclidean geometry and land ownership.

The essay describes the English renaming of

longs for

the living world.

the resurrection of the dolls

decisions will not alight on your shoulder like butterflies
& neither will butterflies
my elders
cement face & I curled up
in our household linen

ccccccccccccccccccccccccccccccccccccccccccccccccccccccccccccccc
ccccccccccccccccccccccccccccccccccccccccccccccvvvvvvvvvvvvvvvv
vvvvvvvvvvvvvvvvvvvvvvvvvvvvvvvvvvvvvvvvvvvvvvvvvvvvvvvvvvv
vvvvvvvvvvvvvvvvvvvvvvvvvvvvvvvvvvvvvvvvvvvvvvvvvvvvvvvvvvv
vvvvvvvvvvvvvvvvvvvvvmmmmmmmmmmmmmmmmmmmmm
mvvvvvvvvvvvvvvvvvvvvvvvvvvvvvvvvvvvvvvvvvvvvvvvvvvvvvvvv
vvvvvvvvvvvvvvvvvvvvvvvvvvvvvvvvvvvvvvvvvvvvvvvvvvvvvvvvvvv
vvvvvvvvvvvvvvv

call me ella

the sweet weight of your daughter in your arms, do you worry?

dream of wiping clots and pools of your own blood from linoleum
while falling in love with your secret service agent apropos of
a few kind remarks from the other side of the stall

dream of supervising steam-cleaning of thick dusty gray carpets
by your terrorist servants while explaining that you, too,
disagree with your government's policies

dream of your daughter dancing in the small muddy waves
in a too-long heavy skirt and too-loose flat maryjanes—
when do you rush in to save her?

and the sweet heavy weight of your daughter in your arms,
as you are kicking at the crowds that rush in from the sea,
do you then worry about retrieving the second shoe (maryjane),
which is turning from pink to mud to stark black (like grandma's
hair) with white (like grandma's hair) embroidery or do you just
let her wear her great-grandmother's purple leaf?

anonymous compline

we've all kind of in
the same spot been

compline at the cavour

unadministered losses behind the wind
a road down from heaven had to be made

(the thornier it is the more religious)

figurehead sea trope

waterbird & skirt fragment
word-bird old as the seas
skirt fragment old as a figurehead

crèche

I'd meant to solve the universal her,
and here I've been a wreck
sometimes and sometimes ambling
up a firm familiar mountain or the seas
to small geographies unmeasured
and unmapped, you'll find them

Grle

as the bright bright day

and I try so hard to hang on to hope it makes my head crack,
and all is just thinking, and thoughts crushing each other,
and forgetting to breathe, and to watch with you, and to walk
with you, and to talk with you, as the green iridescence, as the
almost-too purple, as the bright bright day, as the puddle this
day, and the sun.

pigeon-chasing compline

neighbor spider,
the sun is crying
a moon for every city
a treasure in the tall grass
these birds in a tree

"are we gentlemen?"
                    said Ivy

"am I a lassie?"
"what does the moon say? hello! what does the sun say? hello
says the moon, hi says the sun. Hi moon says Ivy. Hello say the
sun and moon. Hi moon and sun say Ivy and Mama. Hi Ivy and
Mama say the moon and the sun."

starling compline

"They learn new motifs and embed them in their songs."
—Timothy Gentner

> *Just like a* Bird, *when her* Young *are in Nest,*
> *Goes in, and out, and hops and takes no Rest;*
> *But when their* Young *are fledg'd, their heads out peep,*
> *Lord what a chirping does the* Old *one keep.*
> — Margaret Cavendish, Duchess of Newcastle

in the shape of a meadowlark the moon is singing

*

at the fair:

one by one or staggered twos
tough tiny white balloons
scurry up a tall flat blue
crisp streams a-trailing

homesong:

oh daughter thou shalt have to know the too-bright sun,
new fuel econ., the household rain. oh daughter thou
in these sweet days the bomb etc.

my days long gone i'm
true to you in this i swear in this i pray

greensleeves my fears most please allay

happy happy shall you be, dressed like the sea
the rose-up sea, as the skies they flust, and the ice sheets slide
we all change shape, we best our boast, in fear of ye,
whichever how.

greensleeves my daughter ties me still unto this earth, my lessons
kempt, my grace please let

greensleeves my daughter she
explores does you, your dirty dirt, your sooty built,
your city weeds . . . and just today, nasturtium
bird clutched dandelion

the time is come to be grown up

> *The water is wide, I cannot cross o'er*
> *and neither have I wings to fly*
> *give me a boat that can carry two*
> *and both shall row, my child and I*
> *my child and I—*
> —Traditional

at the fair:

her father, in jumpy silver, sings

*

in the shape of a meadowlark the moon is

***

oh daughter thou
shalt grounde and playe
in these sweet days

in these sweet days

Notes

In "The false transgressive evangelista" the following phrases are quotes or misquotes from others: "the birds humming/and the birds not humming" (my niece Violet Treadwell Hull, at age 4); "under the bone tree" (James Thomas Stevens, at Small Press Traffic, 10/04); "by the dinghy" (in salute to my nephew Isaac Treadwell Hull, at age 3, who likes dinghies); "his thousand petticoats" (Rob Halpern, at Small Press Traffic, 11/04); & "the country moon" (unspoken communication with my daughter Ivy Rae Jackson, while reading a picture book, at age 17 months). The poem was partly inspired by Sarah Anne Cox's poem "Unequaled," which she wrote in 2002-03 while we were both pregnant; it began in the margins of my datebook during my daughter's first months.

I started writing "Sonora" at the suggestion of Juliana Spahr for the *Chain 12* dialogue on resource use. I chose this topic because of my relationship with the Sonora through family migration and settling. (For example, my maternal grandmother lived in Tucson, Arizona for roughly the second half of the 20th century, having moved there from Oklahoma in the late 1940s on account of my mother's asthma.) Source texts: The Nature Conservancy's "Population and Conservation in the Sonoran Desert" in the *AAAS Atlas of Population and Environment* (available at http://atlas. aaas.org); *Snapped on the Street: A Community Archive of Photos and Memories from Downtown Tucson 1937-1963*, ed. Farley et al (Tucson, AZ: Tucson Voices Press, 1999); and the Arizona-Sonora Desert Museum website (desertmuseum.org).

"Trod." refers to the Treadwell mansion in Oakland, which an indirect ancestor lost gambling.

"Mamie" refers to my maternal great-grandmother from Oklahoma.

"The imported ghost deer of Inverness, California" came after a brief conversation with Beverly Dahlen.

"Sourgrass" is after Robert Pinsky's poem about people dreaming in Berkeley.

The epigram for "In Cloudland" is taken from a description of Mrs. Musgrave's Victorian fairy tale *In Cloudland* (London: Blackie & Son, 1891?) on Violet Books (violetbooks.com/gal-fairy2.html). The poem is co-written by Violet Treadwell Hull.

"mub" — some words from "Bird Brains Get Some New Names, And New Respect" by Rick Weiss, which appeared in *The Washington Post* February 1, 2005 and was posted to the Buffalo Poetics Listserv by Miekal And.

"Buffalo 3000" written from google for "ladyless" and other sources July 5, 2005, as part of preparing to speak & read in Buffalo in November 2005.

"gelatin" — words from the FibroGen website and Katie Whitaker's biography of Margaret (Lucas) Cavendish, Duchess of Newcastle, *Mad Madge* (New York: Basic Books, 2003). My title, *Birds & Fancies*, is after Cavendish's 1653 book, *Poems, and Fancies*.

I got the following titles from American *Vogue*: "The Carnation Skirt" (July 2005), "the resurrection of the dolls" (May 2006), and "call me ella" (May 2006).

"The Carnation Skirt" — I cowrote the section "brown" with my daughter Ivy Rae Jackson (29 months) on November 1, 2005. It is dedicated with love to my third conceived baby, whom I miscarried in September 2005.

"Pink druzy"'s spitting out of ancient names I misheard from Sarah Anne Cox.

"Temporary" includes a phrase each from my niece Violet (6 yrs) (she was drawing a "haunted dress" one day, and then added an inhabitant) and my daughter Ivy Rae (34 months) ("the other moons" as well as the eyes like planets, rather than stars, concept). It's also informed by J. B. Harley's essay, "New England Cartography and the Native Americans" and the anonymous c. 1584 poem "A new Courtly Sonet, of the Lady Greensleeves. To the new tune of Greensleeves," and by the aforementioned tune.

"Foursquare compline" written for the inaugural issue of *Foursquare*.

"Blogosphere compline" — the "lumpy clouds" are from Elisa Kleven's *Sun Bread*.

"compline at the cavour" — thorny observation belongs to Violet Treadwell Hull.

"are we gentlemen?" — recorded to the best of my ability over two evenings, the poem was composed by Ivy Rae Jackson.

"starling compline" — begun in response to "Starlings' Listening Skills May Shed Light on Language Evolution" by Carl Zimmer, which appeared in *The New York Times* May 2, 2006 and was posted to the Discussion of Women's Poetry Listserv by Kim Becker. The phrase "the moon is singing" belongs to Ivy Rae Jackson.

Printed in the United States
62796LVS00002B/1-33

9 781905 700165